**This book is to be returned on or before
the last date stamped below.**

LIBREX

516

Holes

Written by Paul Bennett

Wayland

Picture acknowledgements

The publishers would like to thank the following for allowing their photographs to be reproduced in this book: Bruce Coleman Ltd. 6 (above/Eric Crichton), 6 (below/Geoff Dore), 12 (Jane Burton), 13 (below/Andrew Purcell), 14 (above/G.D. Plage), 14 (below/Kim Taylor), 15 (above/Stephen J. Krasemann), 15 (below/Leonard Lee Rue), 18 (below/Adrian Davies); Chris Fairclough 10 (top), 17 (above and below), 23 (both), 24 (above); Sally and Richard Greenhill 4 (above), 29; Tony Stone Worldwide *title page*, 25; Eye Ubiquitous 4 (below/Paul Seheult), 8 (Simon Punter), 11 (Roger Chester), 16 (Paul Seheult); Wayland Picture Library 5, 9 (both), 20, 21 (above), 22, 26 (below), 28; Tim Woodcock 10 (middle and below), 24 (below), 27; ZEFA 7, 13 (above), 18 (above), 19, 21, 26 (above).

**Cover photography by Zul Mukhida, organized by Zoë Hargreaves.
With thanks to Stanford Infants School.**

First published in 1992 by
Wayland (Publishers) Ltd
61 Western Road, Hove
East Sussex BN3 1JD, England

© Copyright 1992 Wayland (Publishers) Ltd

Editor: Francesca Motisi
Designers: Jean and Robert Wheeler
Picture research: Paul Bennett

Consultant: Norah Granger is a senior lecturer in Early Years Education Studies for teacher training courses at Brighton Polytechnic. She was formerly the headteacher of a primary school in West Sussex and has primary and nursery teaching experience in East Sussex and Inner London. Norah wrote the notes for parents and teachers and provided the topic web.

British Library Cataloguing in Publication Data
Bennett Paul.
Holes. – (Criss cross)
I. Title II. Series
155.4

ISBN 0-7502-0402-8

Typeset by DJS Fotoset Ltd, Brighton, Sussex
Printed and bound in Italy by L.E.G.O. S.p.A., Vicenza

Contents

Words that appear in **bold** in the text are explained in the glossary on page 32.

What is a hole?

There are many different kinds of holes.

You can dig a hole. Have you ever dug a hole using a spade?

This dog is digging a hole.

4

You can put things into holes.
A bowl has a hole you can pour water into.

Natural holes

Some holes are made by nature. The waves in the sea can make holes in cliffs.

Some plants have leaves with holes in them. This tree has a hole in its bark.

Sometimes you can see the moon through a hole in the clouds. Have you seen any natural holes?

Making holes

Many holes are made by people. A drill is used to make a hole in a piece of wood.

Tunnels are holes cut through a hill or under the ground. Trains and cars go through a tunnel to pass under a river or through a mountain.

This is a coal mine in Australia. It is a huge hole! The **miners** get the coal out of the ground by using big machines.

Windows and doors

Many holes are **openings**.
A window is an opening to let ▶
the light through into a room.

When you open a
◀ door, you can go
through a hole in
the wall.

You go through a
doorway to get on ▶
to a bus.

10

Have you opened any doors today
so that you can go through a hole?

Animal homes

This rabbit lives in a hole called a burrow.
It keeps the rabbit safe from the wind and rain,
and from enemies.

Many birds make nests in holes. This owl is nesting in a hole in a tree.

Here is a mole coming out of his home. Moles dig tunnels under the ground.

This white lady
spider is coming
out of the tunnel
it is digging.
It lives in the
Namib Desert in
West Africa.

This grub is coming out of a hole that it has eaten
in a nut. Eventually the grub will change into a
type of beetle called a weevil.

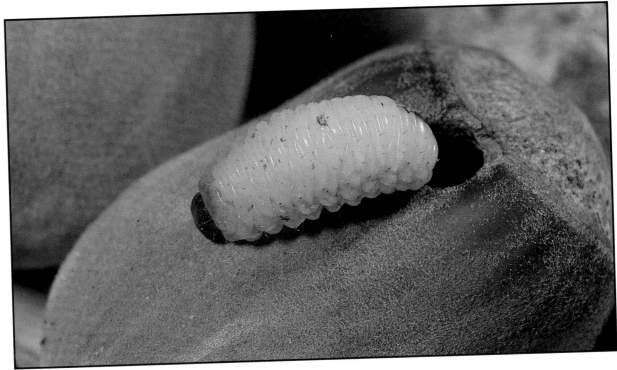

This seal from Canada is called a harp seal. When the water is frozen, seals have to come up for air, through holes in the ice.

People often provide boxes for birds to nest in. This bird-box has a hole just big enough for a tree swallow to get in and out.

Holes for hands

Scissors have holes for your fingers to go through. This helps you to hold the scissors when you cut things.

Boxes often have holes. The holes can be used as handles, so that the boxes can be picked up and moved around.

The handle on a cup makes a hole for your fingers.

What else do you have at home with a hole that makes a handle?

Holes for water

Taps and **hoses** have holes to let the water through.

A water **sprinkler** has many little holes to send out a spray ▶ of water.

These children are finding out what lives in the pond. The net has holes in it to let the water run out. ▼

Useful holes

This market **stall** has lots of useful things with holes, such as bowls and bottles. How many other things like these can you see?

Straws are tubes with ▶ holes at both ends. You can suck up the drink through the holes in the straw.

◀ Many kitchen tools have holes. Some of them have holes in their handles so that they can be hung up on hooks.

Look around your home and see how many useful things you can find with holes in them.

Holes in clothes

Your clothes have holes for your head, hands and feet. Without these holes you would not be able to put your clothes on, or put things in your pockets.

Some holes are for doing up your clothes, like these buttonholes.

These holes are in a belt. The **buckle** goes through a hole to fasten the belt.

23

Making music

Can you play a musical instrument? Some musical instruments have holes so that you can make the sounds.

You blow into a hole in a recorder to make a sound. There are holes for your fingers, so that you can make high and low sounds.

◀ Instruments with strings have holes too. The holes help to make the sound.

This instrument is called a ▶ euphonium. It has a very big hole to let out a loud sound!

Fun with holes

Blowing bubbles is fun! The hole you blow through makes the bubbles.

Have you ever rolled up a piece of paper to make a tube? You can look through it like a **telescope**.

26

This boy is cutting shapes out of pastry.
You can see the holes left in the pastry.

Patterns

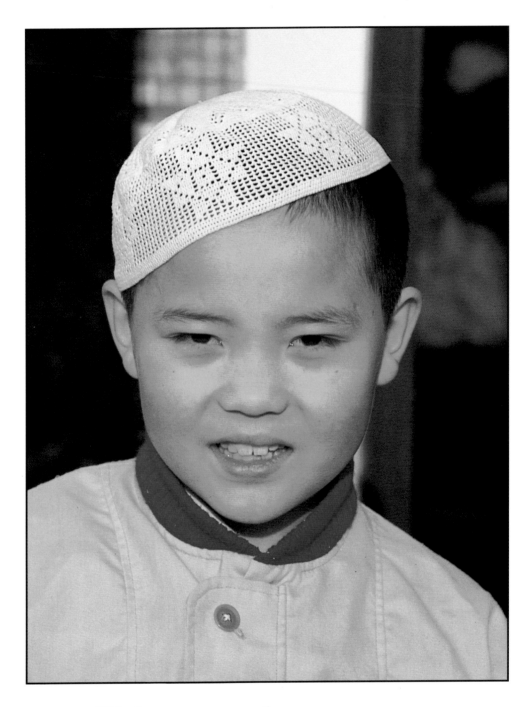

Holes can make patterns.
This boy is wearing a cap with
a pattern made by holes.

These children are making patterns by
threading wool through holes in paper.
Look for other patterns that holes make.

Notes for parents and teachers

Through experimenting, observing and discussing, children can be encouraged to consider the variety of holes both natural and made by people, and the ways in which objects with holes can be used. Investigations of this kind can help children in the early years to acquire skills in experimenting, observing and recording. Language can be enriched and extended through the need to discuss observations, communicate ideas, pose questions and use new words.

Some suggestions for classifying objects with holes
- Holes that separate things – nets, sieves, colanders, graters, sifters.
- Holes that things go through – taps, hoses, tubes, handles, rings, funnels, tunnels, buttonholes, needles, sand clock.
Holes to put things in – cups, buckets, bowls, bottles, cartons.
- Things that close up holes – doors, windows, flaps, corks, lids, buttons, zips, eyelids, valves.
- Creatures that live in holes – rabbits, badgers, foxes, moles, birds, snails, worms, ants.
- Holes for sounds – whistles, mouths, ears, recorders, trumpets, telephones.
- Tools that make holes – needles, spades, screwdrivers, spoons, trowels, mechanical diggers, fingers.

Some suggestions for activities
Levels of experimenting and recording can be varied to suit the needs and developing skills of the children. First steps might be exploratory play, progressing to the need for fair testing with, for example, measured quantities, methods of timing, considering variables.

In and out of holes
- Observing speed of water flow from: containers with wide and narrow tops/openings; containers with different sizes and numbers of holes in or made in them.
- Testing ease of filling containers with wide and narrow openings, and finding ways to overcome problems found e.g. plastic and paper funnels.
- Making water come out in very small amounts – vinegar bottle dropper, eye dropper, washing up liquid bottle.
- Testing best tool shapes for digging small and large holes in sand/soil-stick, spoon, scoop, trowel, fork, spade.

Straining and filtering
- Testing effects of materials with different sized holes.
- Testing effects of different sized spaces between varying sized particles – straining water from grains of different sizes through colander, sieve, nylon stocking, muslin, paper.
- Filtering water from soil using the above – how is water purified?
- Make simple filters with two perforated plastic tubs placed over jam jars. Half fill one tub with clean sand and the other with clean stones. Top up tubs with muddy water. Compare results.

Holes for sorting
- Making sorting machines: separate and sort grains of varying size in a tissue box with holes made in the base. A range of boxes of graduating hole size could be made.
- Sort small marbles from larger ones in a V-shaped card shute. Make a hole half way down for the small marbles to fall through into a box and the larger marbles to roll into a box at the end of the chute.

Letting light through holes
- Look at shapes, sizes and position of windows.
- Experiment with slits and cut-out shapes in card to see how much light comes through and how much you can see through them when held up to the eye.
- Make a simple pin-hole theatre from a shoe box. Cut away a third of the lid at one end and cover the hole with coloured tissue paper or cellophane. At the opposite end make a small eye hole in the short side of the box. A backdrop picture can be fixed inside the box at the opposite end to the eye hole. Card figures can be fixed inside at varying distances from the eyehole to make a scene.
- Look inside a real camera and watch the shutter action and effects of altering the aperture setting.
- Look at eye pupils as holes for light. Observe effects of different amounts of light.

Holes in fabrics and papers
Examine fabric structure against a light source, or with a magnifying glass. Look for the closeness of the weave and the size and shape of holes.

- Tie fabrics over jars and test how much and how fast water passes through.
- Observe water resistance in relation to hole size (loose and tight weave).
- Try weaving – paper, ribbon, grasses, string.
- Test water absorption in materials with different size holes – types of paper, sponges, fabrics.
- Test effects of paper with different size holes used as water filters – tea bags, coffee filters.

Holes for catching sounds
- Make and test paper cone trumpets and speaking tubes using rubber tubing with squeezy bottle/yoghurt pot ends.
- Experiment with a stethoscope.
- Experiment with sea-shells – the shape of the cavity catches the sounds made inside the ear and amplifies them.
- Make musical instruments from card tubes, bottles containing different amounts of water.

Holes and air pressure
- Experiment with paper parachutes. Do they work better with holes in the chutes?
- Look at a bicycle pump. How does it work?
- What makes a blown up balloon fly backwards when released?

Holes to live in
- Observe and discuss the kinds of animals, birds and insects that make and use holes as homes. How are nests constructed and why are they 'lined'? Consider, protection from weather and enemies, food stores, needs of young.
- Pictures of cross-sections of burrows can show the structures and networks of the tunnels which lie beyond the holes we can see.
- Minibeasts – make a temporary ant home. Fill a large jam jar with loamy soil and cover the top with muslin and the sides with black paper. Feed ants on sugar lumps and apple pieces. After about a week the children will be able to see the tunnels the ants have made.

Making patterns with holes
- Experiment with repeating printed patterns using cut vegetables.
- Cutting and tearing holes in folded paper to make symmetrical patterns.
- Making paper/card masks with different shaped eye, nose, mouth holes.
- Look at perforations in paper and their uses – stamps, tear-off forms.

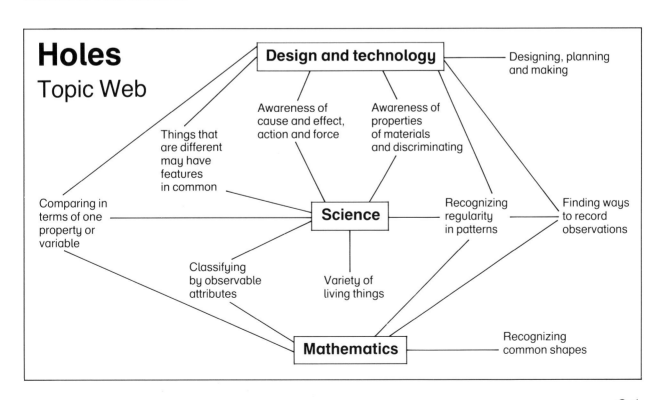

Glossary

Buckle A fastening on a belt or shoe.

Hoses Pipes that can be bent easily without breaking. Hoses are often used for watering the garden.

Miners People who work in the ground digging for such things as coal and iron.

Openings A gap or hole for letting things go through.

Sprinkler Something that scatters (throws about) water in different directions.

Stall A small stand in a market for selling things.

Telescope An object used for looking at things which are far away. It makes them look bigger and nearer.

Index